Come to the

Celebrate Malay Muslim Festivals

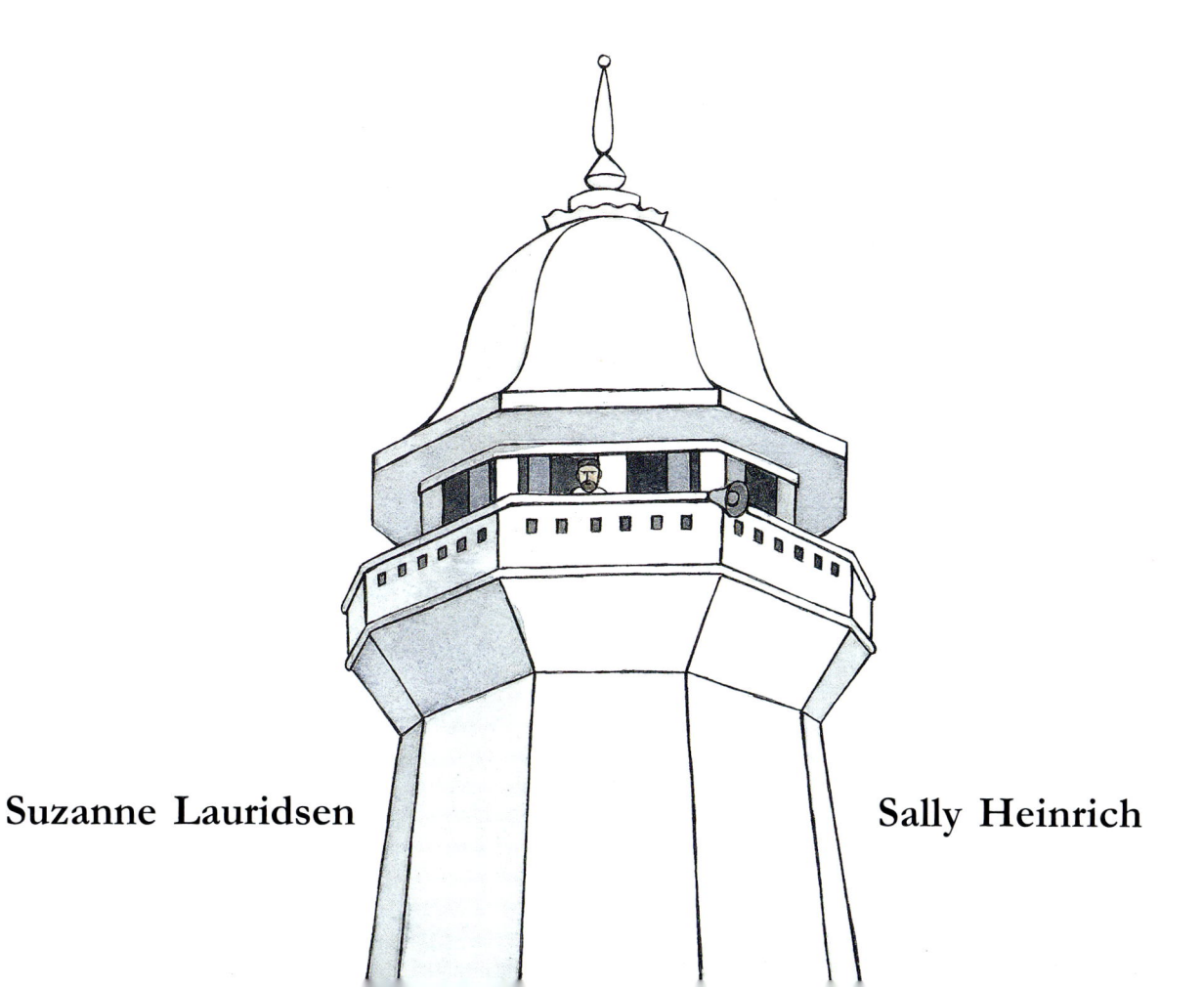

Suzanne Lauridsen
Sally Heinrich

Festivals tend to evolve as they travel from place to place. This book does not attempt to portray the definitive versions of Malay Muslim festivals, but merely describe how some of them are celebrated in the Asia-Pacific region.

Hello!
My name is Ahmad.
I am a Muslim.
That means my religion is Islam.
This is my friend, Max.
I am taking him to some Muslim festivals.
You can come, too!

Hello!

Salam sejahtera!

Ramadan

Today is the first day of Ramadan, the ninth month of the Muslim calendar. It's lunchtime.

Max notices that I have no food.

"Here, have some of mine!" he says.

I thank him for the offer but I cannot accept.

You see, almost all Muslim people fast during Ramadan. That means we eat nothing all day from sunrise to sunset.

We do this to show our love for Allah. It also helps us understand what it feels like to be poor and hungry.

Allah: The Muslim name for God.

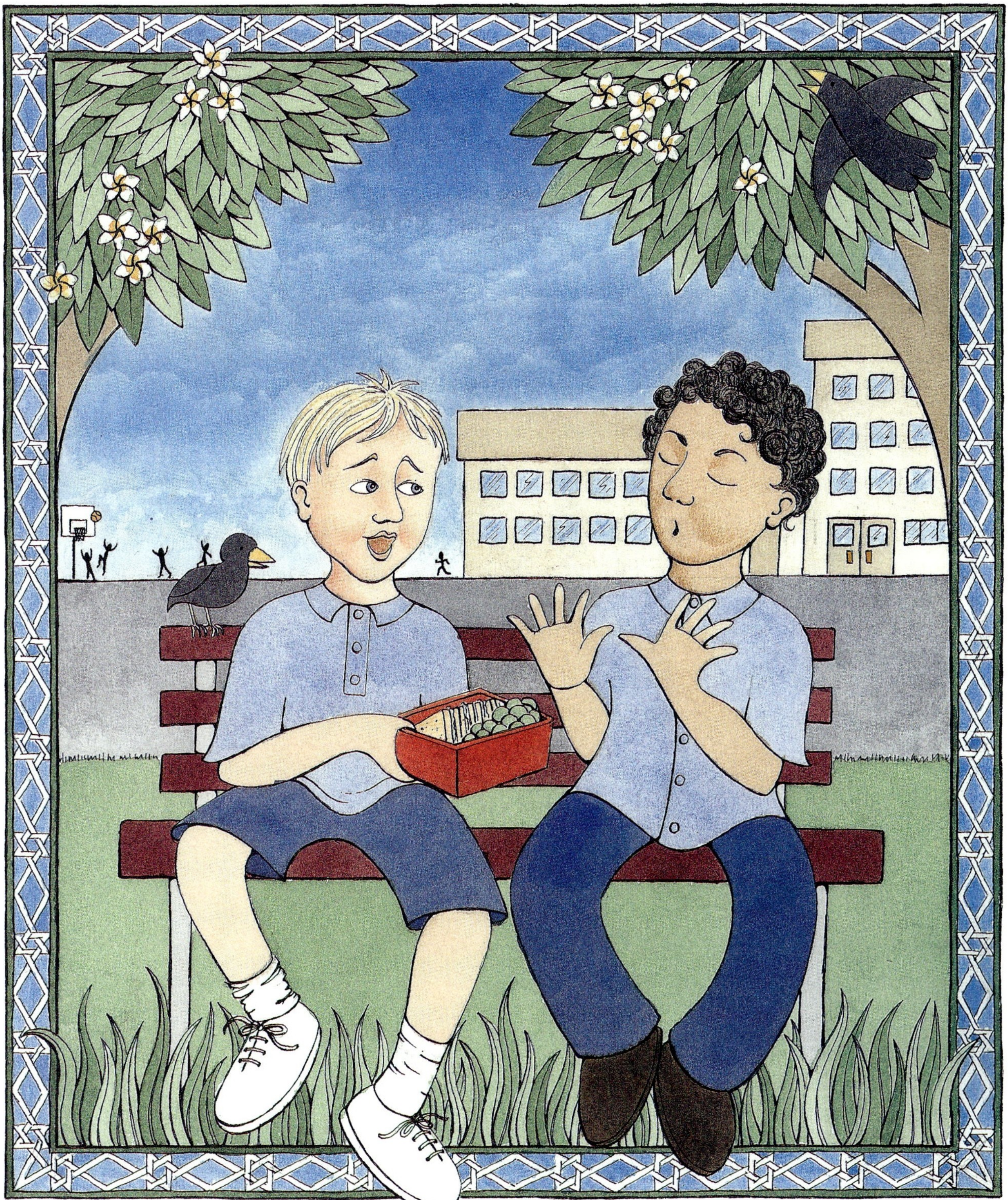

At last the sun has set. It means the fast is over for the day.

First I eat a few dates and drink a glass of water. The little snack gets my tummy ready for the big meal later. Then I say a special prayer.

All Muslim people pray five times a day. We pray in a building called a mosque. We also pray at work or school or home. In fact, we can pray just about anywhere at all.

Mosque: A place where Muslims pray and meet.

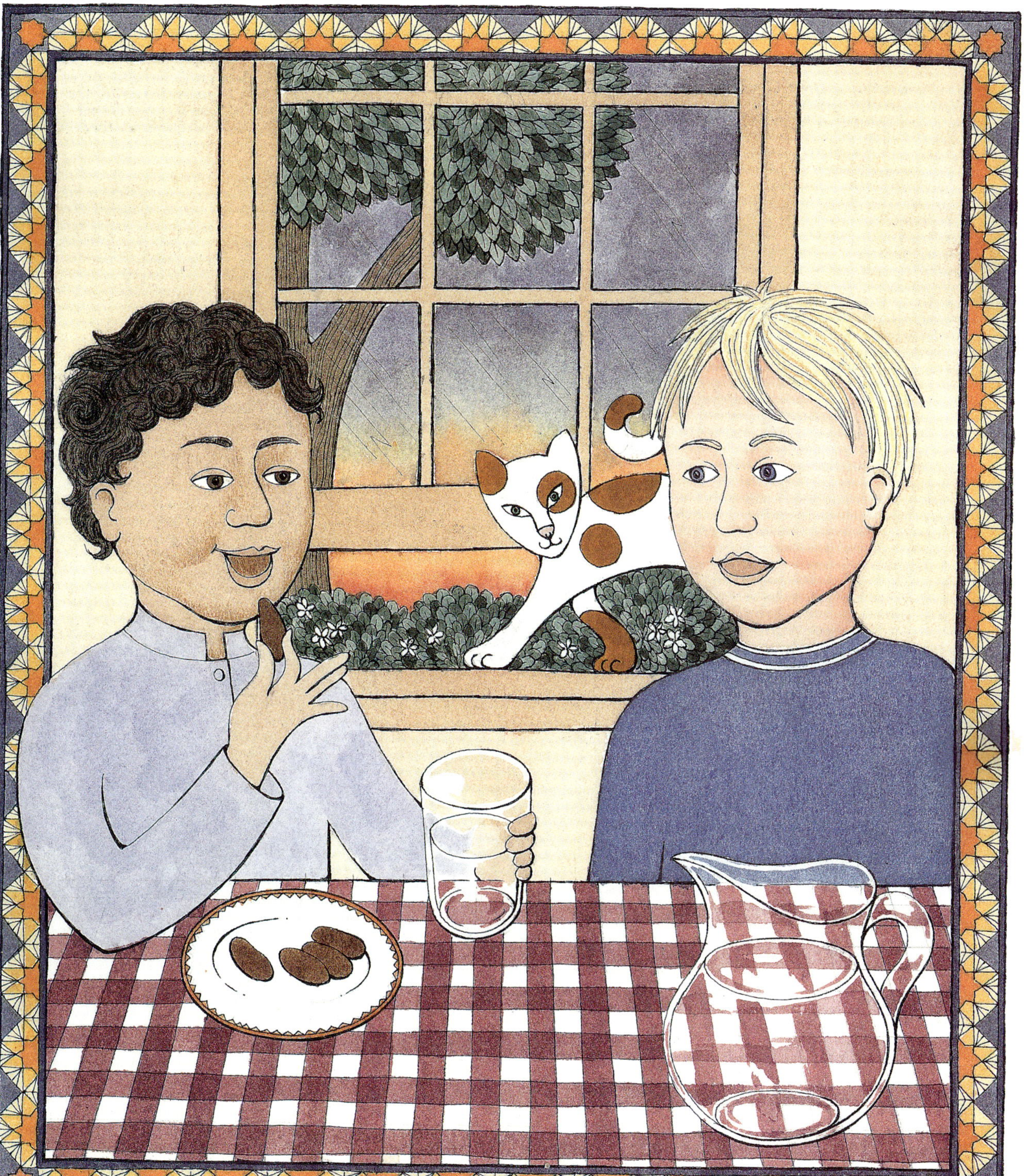

After dark, I take Max to the Malay part of town. See the mosque?

The round roof is called a dome. When you are under it, you feel very calm.

The tower is called a minaret. A man used to climb to the top and call out to remind people when to say their prayers. These days, a recording of the call is often played over loud speakers instead.

We say extra prayers on the nights of Ramadan.

Dome: The rounded roof of a mosque, inspired by the building style of the Middle East.

Minaret: The tower of a mosque from which the call to prayer is sounded.

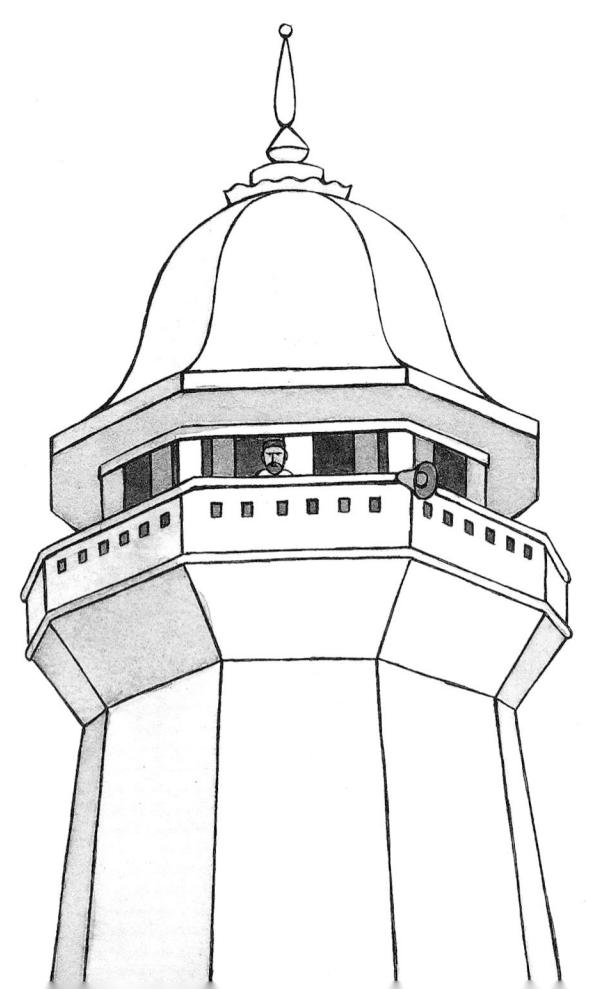

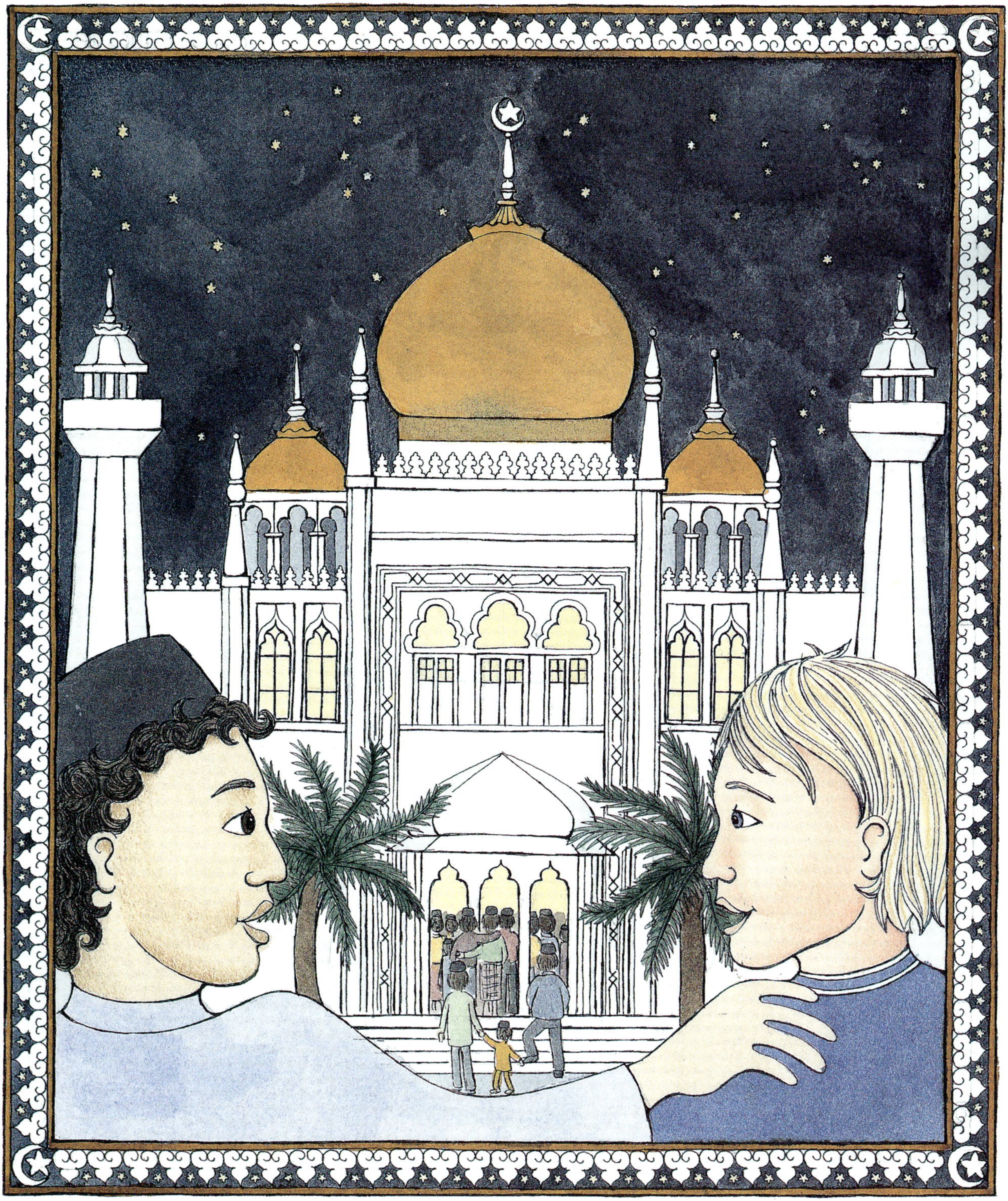

Now we are at the night market. We call it a *pasar malam*. It's open every night during Ramadan.

There is music in the air and everywhere you look there are coloured lights. Little shops along the footpath sell nice new things and all sorts of delicious food. There is no pork for sale, because it is not *halal*.

"Mmm, this *satay* is good. I like the *murtabak* and fried chicken, too," Max says with his mouth full.

But after fasting all day long, everything tastes good to me!

Pasar malam:	A night market, usually set up along a street.
Halal:	Describing foods that are prepared according to Islamic rites.
Satay:	Small pieces of meat barbecued on wooden sticks and eaten with a tasty peanut sauce.
Murtabak:	A type of fried flat bread filled with chicken, mutton or sardines.

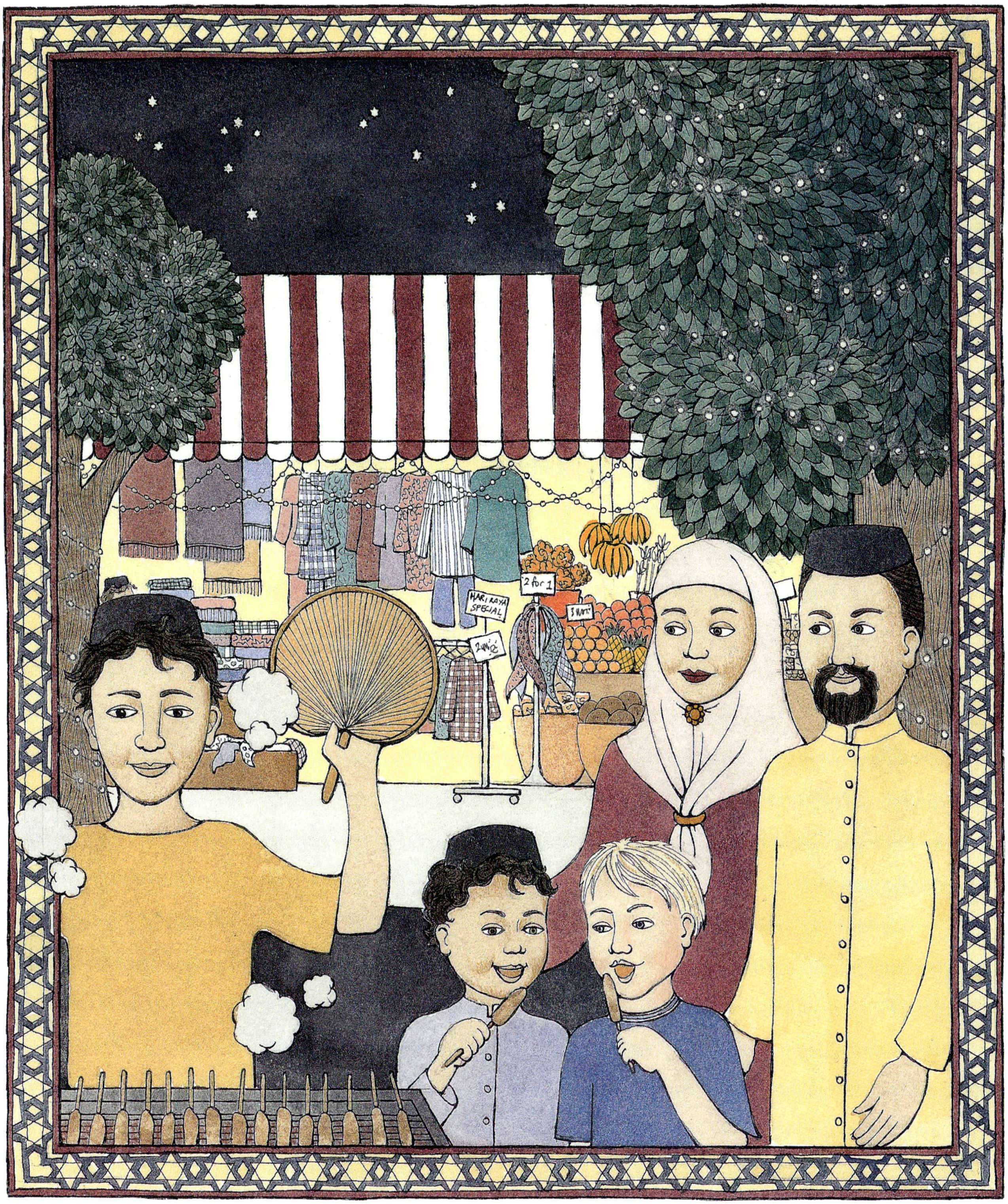
HARI RAYA SPECIAL
2 for 1

Lailatul Qadar

Tonight is Lailatul Qadar, the 27th night of Ramadan. The mosque is so full that the prayer mats touch end to end.

"Why is there such a big crowd tonight?" Max asks.

"Many years ago, on this night, the sky opened up and Allah sent angels down to earth with an important book called the Qur'an," I explain. "They took it to a man named Muhammad, whom Allah had chosen to be His Prophet.

"Now every year on the same night, the sky opens up and angels fly down. They collect all the prayers and rush them straight to Allah!"

Qur'an: The holy book of Islam.
Prophet: The teacher or interpreter of the will of God (Allah).

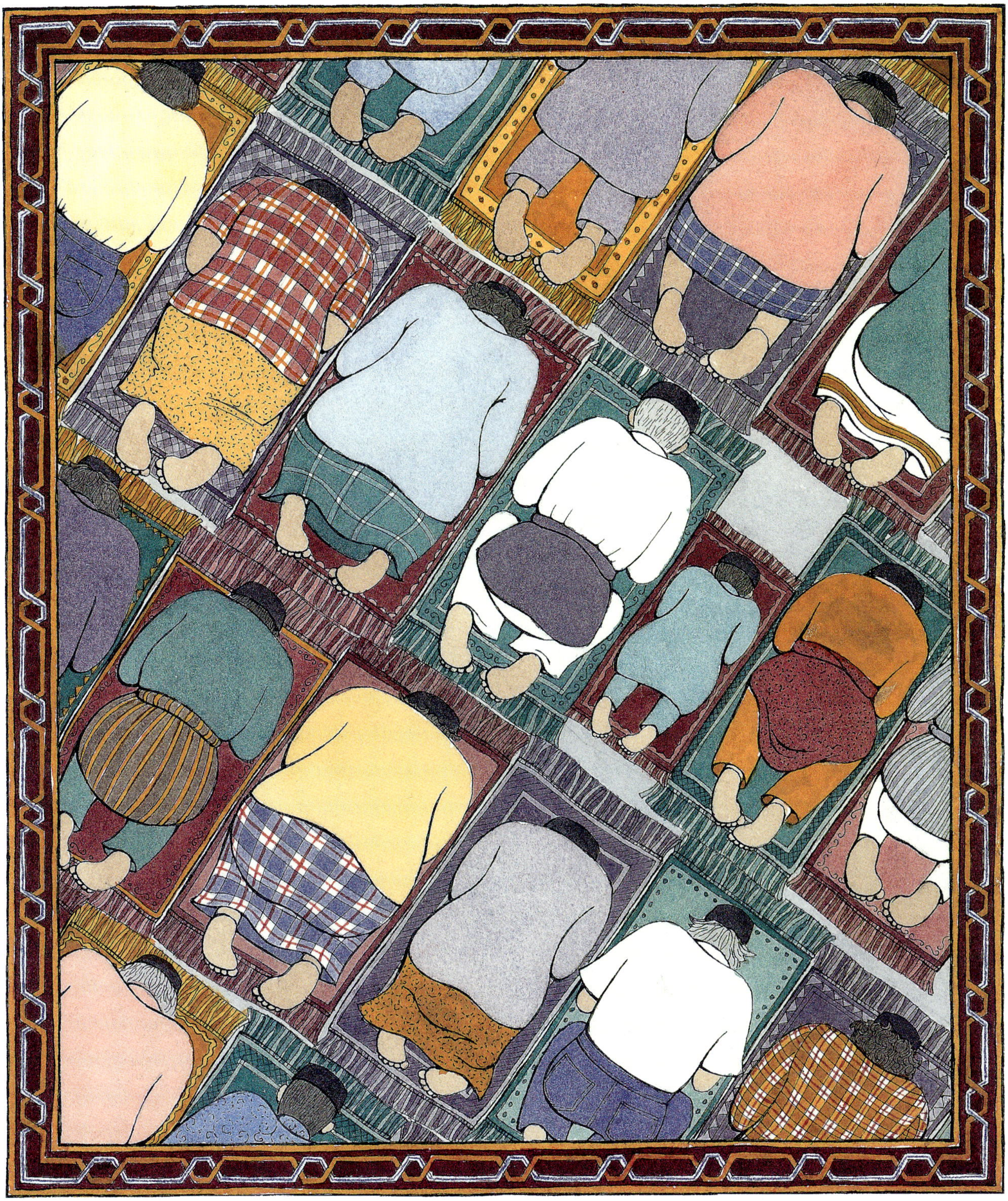

Hari Raya Eidil Fitri

A few days later, there is a tiny new moon in the sky. It means that Ramadan has ended and Hari Raya Eidil Fitri has begun. Some people call it Hari Raya Puasa.

People hug and shake hands. It is time to celebrate and thank Allah for helping us complete the fast.

After a special prayer, we visit our family, friends and neighbours.

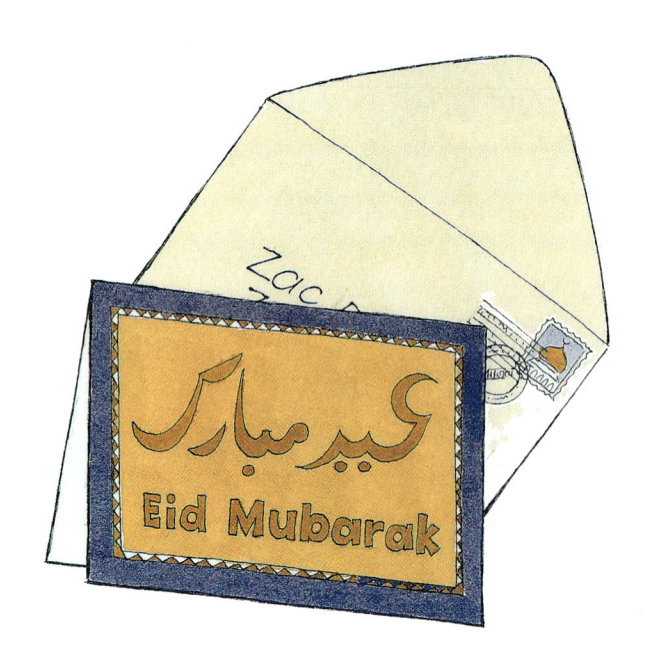

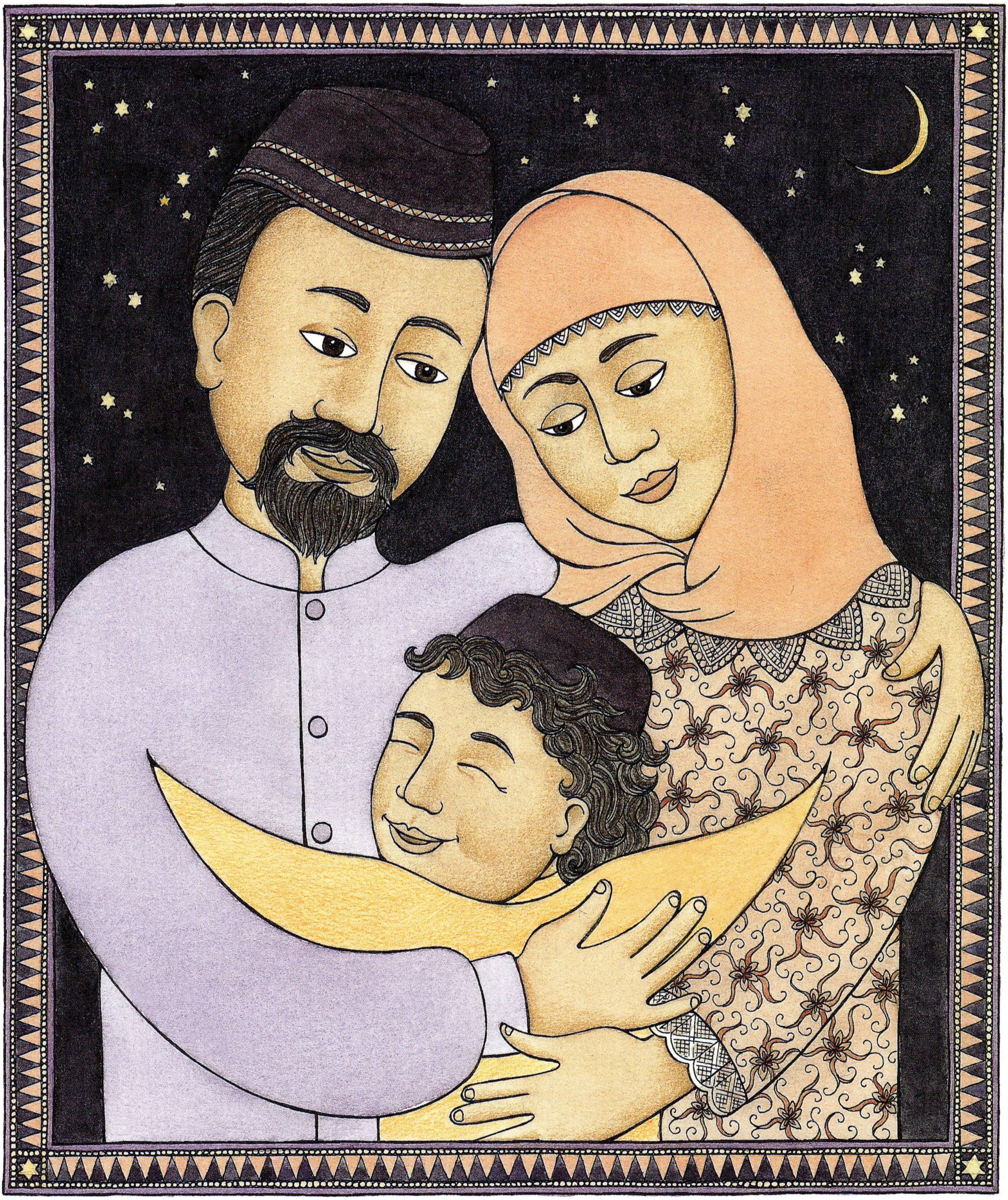

My family celebrates Hari Raya Eidil Fitri with a gathering at our place. It is called an open house, because the door is open and everyone is welcome.

Our house is sparkling clean. We are all dressed up in our finest clothes.

"Hi, Max!" I wave to my friend and take him to meet the other guests.

I greet my Muslim friend, Zakaria, in the traditional way with a *salam*. I shake his hand lightly and then touch my heart.

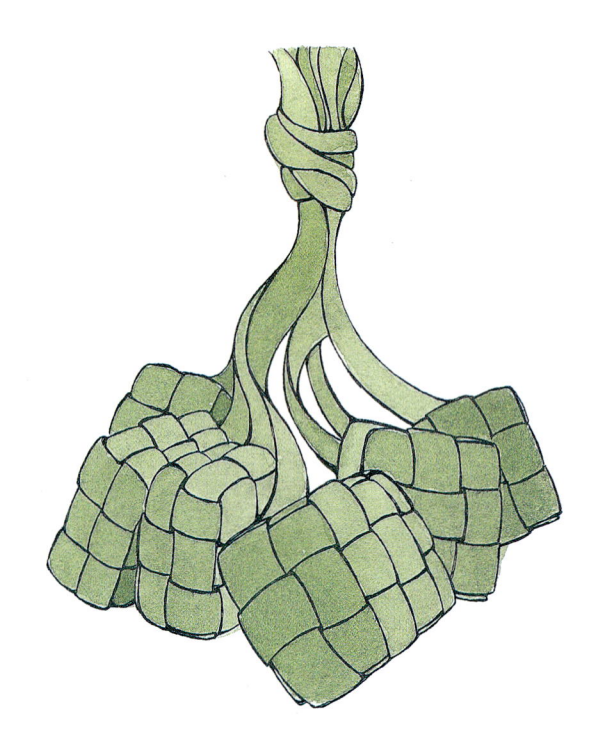

Salam: A traditional Muslim greeting by saying *Assalamu'alaikum* (peace be upon you). Members of the same sex also shake hands.

Selamat Hari Raya Puasa

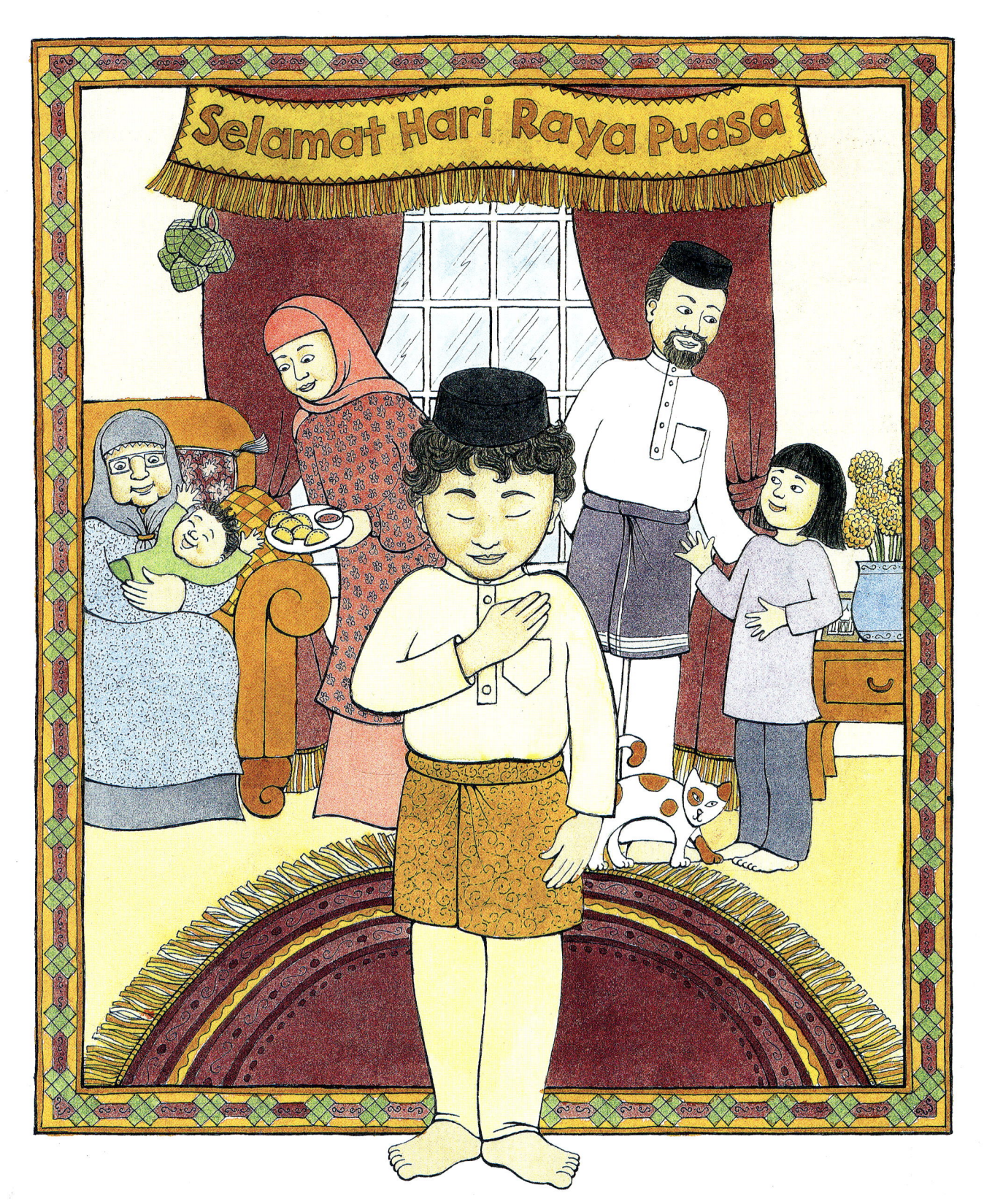

The grown-ups give the children green paper packets with money inside them. Max gets some, too.

There is plenty of wonderful food. Max is not afraid to try spicy dishes. He takes some *lontong,* some *rendang*, and some *sambal goreng.*

But both of us love the cookies most of all!

Lontong:	Rice cakes eaten with coconut gravy.
Rendang:	A spicy beef dish cooked in coconut milk.
Sambal goreng:	A fried vegetable dish with small pieces of beef, liver and lungs.

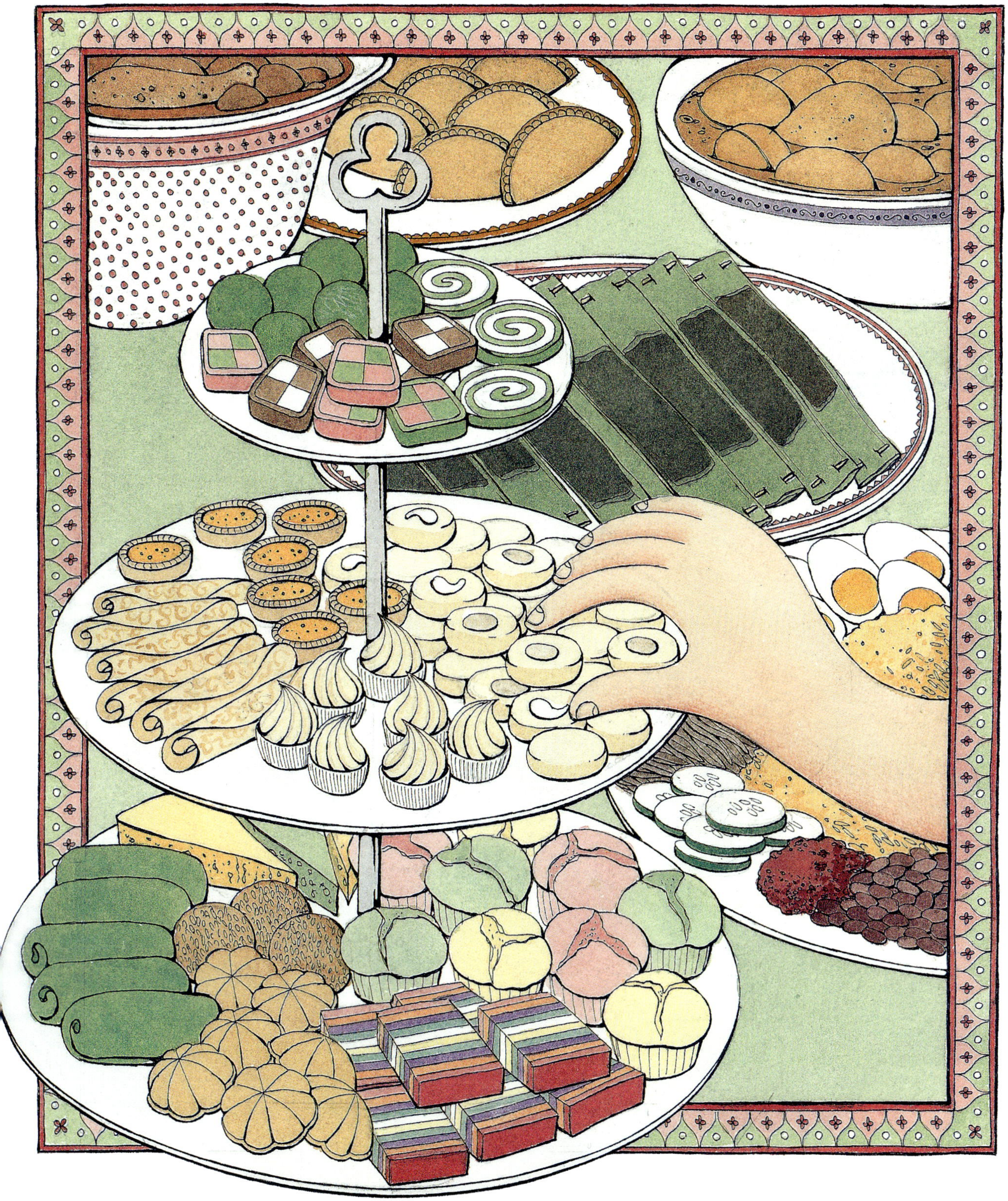

Hari Raya Eidil Adha

We are at the mosque on the morning of Hari Raya Eidil Adha. Some people call it Hari Raya Haji.

"Why is your dad slaughtering a sheep?" Max asks.

"A long time ago, Allah asked a Prophet called Abraham to give Him the life of his son," I explain.

"Even though Abraham loved his son very much, he said yes, because he loved Allah even more. Allah was pleased with Abraham's answer. It was just a test, you see, and Abraham had passed.

"So at the last minute, Allah told Abraham to keep his son and slaughter a goat instead.

"Now every year Muslims slaughter an animal for Allah on Hari Raya Eidil Adha, just like Abraham did. Then we share the meat with poor people."

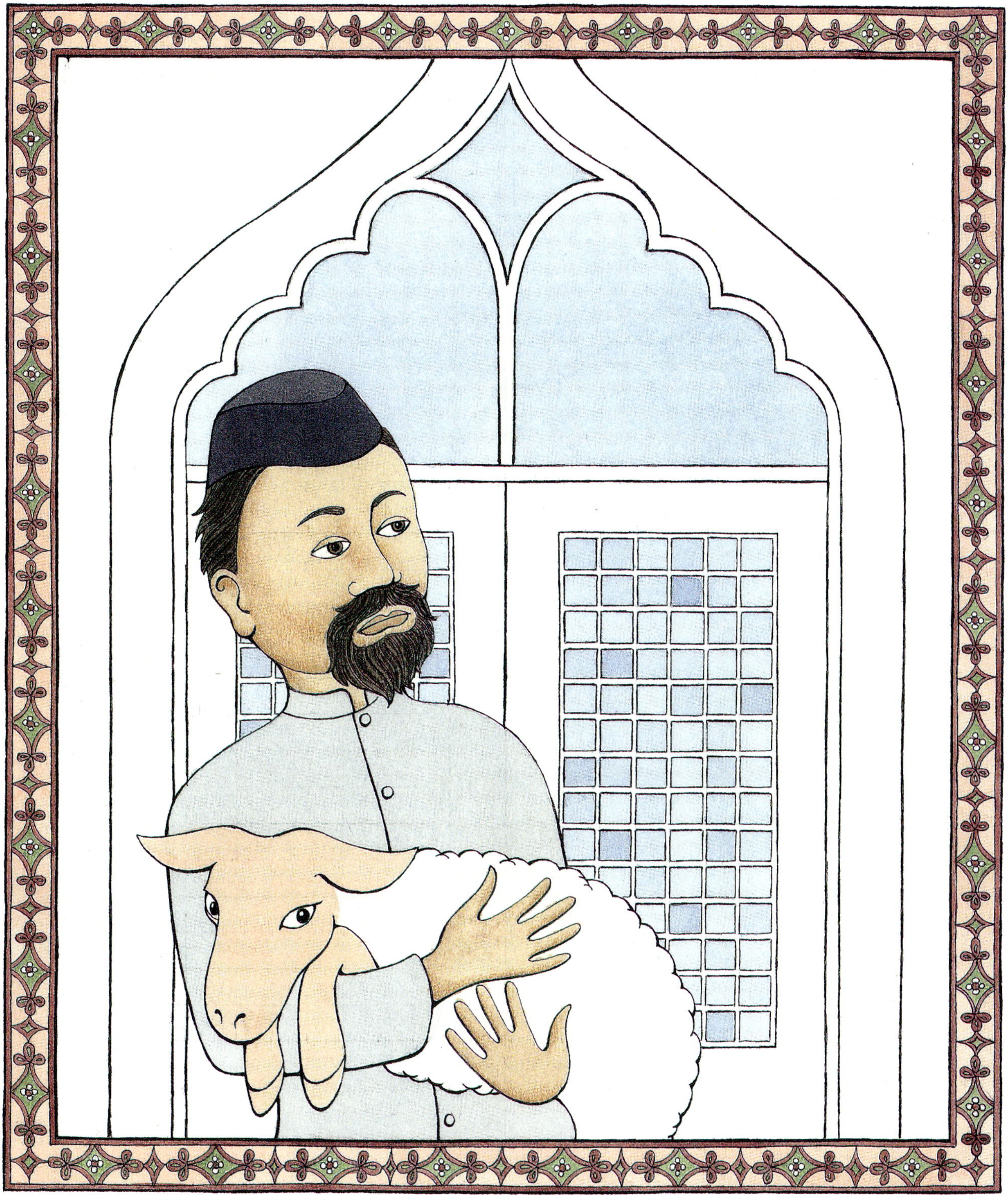

It is the afternoon of Hari Raya Eidil Adha. There is a big feast at the mosque. Everybody is invited. Poor and lonely people are especially welcome. Max is here as my guest.

"Where are your Uncle Rahim and Aunty Sharifah?" asks Max, looking around.

"They've gone on a special trip to a place called Mecca," I reply.

Selamat Hari Raya Haji!

Mecca: The site of the holy Ka'aba and the birthplace of Prophet Muhammad.

Selamat Hari Raya Eidil'Adha

Mecca is a very important place for Muslims. It is where Muhammad was born and the holy Ka'aba stands. We always face the direction of the Ka'aba in Mecca when we pray.

If they have enough money for the trip, all Muslim people must go to Mecca at least once in their life to perform Haj. Many go during Hari Raya Haji.

We switch on the TV. There is a story about Mecca.

"I think I can see Uncle Rahim and Aunty Sharifah!" shouts Max excitedly.

Ka'aba: A cube-shaped shrine at Mecca.
Haj: A pilgrimage (journey made for religious reasons) to Mecca.

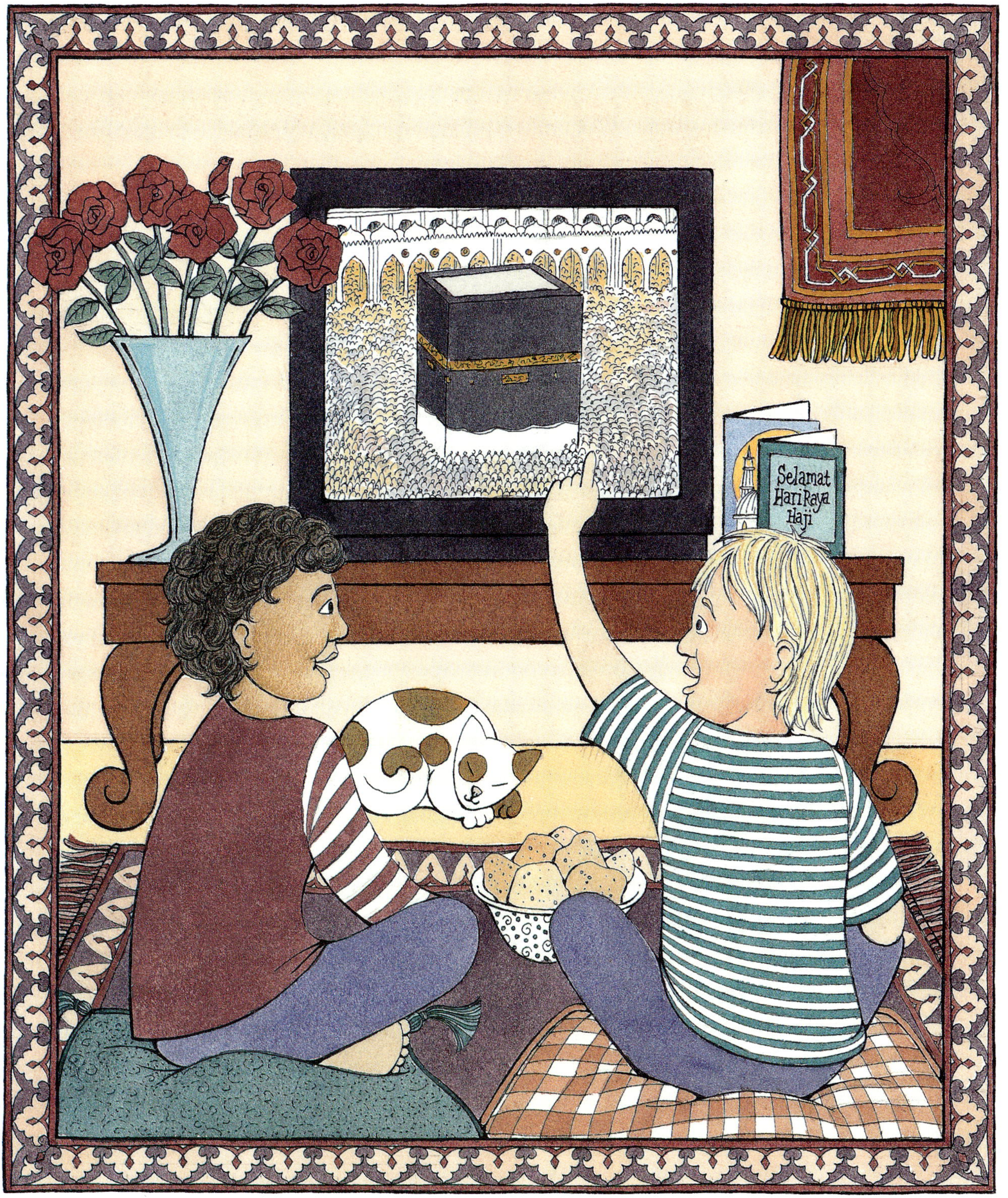
Selamat Hari Raya Haji

I had a great time with Max.
I hope you did, too.

Goodbye! Selamat jalan!

Calendar

The Muslim lunar calendar fixes its dates by the cycles of the moon. As it changes from year to year, no Western dates can be given.

Ramadan is the ninth month of the Muslim lunar calendar.

Lailatul Qadar is the 27th night of Ramadan. Sometimes it refers to the final ten days.

Hari Raya Eidil Fitri, also known as Hari Raya Puasa, is the first day of the tenth month of the Muslim lunar calendar.

Hari Raya Eidil Adha, also known as Hari Raya Haji, takes place in Zulhijjah. Zulhijjah is the twelfth month of the Muslim lunar calendar.

Time Line

Hang a large long piece of paper on the wall, divided into twelve parts — one for each month of the year. Label the months. Then mark the major Malay Muslim festivals as they occur throughout the year. You can mark other festivals too.

Hold a Quiz

Ask the children to raise their hand if they know the answers to the following questions.

1. What do Muslim people do from sunrise to sunset during Ramadan?
2. What kind of meat are Muslims not allowed to eat?
3. What is the special sign that Ramadan has ended and Hari Raya Eidil Fitri (or Hari Raya Puasa) has begun?
4. What is the name of the building where Muslim people go to pray?
5. What is the special name for the tower of a mosque?
6. Who was asked by Allah to slaughter his son?
7. Who received the Qur'an from Allah?
8. What do Muslim people face when they pray?
9. How do Malay Muslim males greet each other?
10. How do Malay Muslims celebrate Hari Raya Eidil Fitri?

Answer: 1) They fast. 2) Pork. 3) A tiny new moon appears in the sky. 4) A mosque. 5) A minaret. 6) Abraham. 7) Muhammad. 8) The Ka'aba in Mecca. 9) They perform the salam by shaking hands and touching their heart. 10) With an open house.

Make up a Story

Tell a story about 'A Day In The Life Of A Malay Boy/Girl'. Start it off along the lines of: "Hello, my name is Aida. I am seven years old and I live in a *kampung*..." Then go round the room, asking each person to add a sentence. See where the story takes you!

Go on an Outing

Go to a Malay restaurant and eat some Malay food. Visit your local mosque.

Make a Mosque Collage

Materials: Large sheet of paper (white, sky-blue or night sky-black). Coloured paper. Scissors. Glue.

Instructions: After your visit to a mosque, draw its outline onto a piece of paper, remembering the distinctive shapes of the dome and minaret (tower). Cut out the mosque and stick it onto a large sheet of paper. Decorate your collage. You can use the printing block (next page) to print a border.

Make a Printing Block

Materials: Piece of thick cardboard, approximately 4 cm x 6 cm (or proportionately larger). Pencil (for drawing pattern). Thick string. Glue and scissors. Liquid paint (for printing).

Instructions: Draw a geometric design on the cardboard. Glue string over the drawn line. When glue is dry, dip printing block in paint and press on paper to print borders and patterns.

Note: Islamic (Muslim) art is always non-representative. That means it never shows images of actual people or things, only abstract geometric patterns.

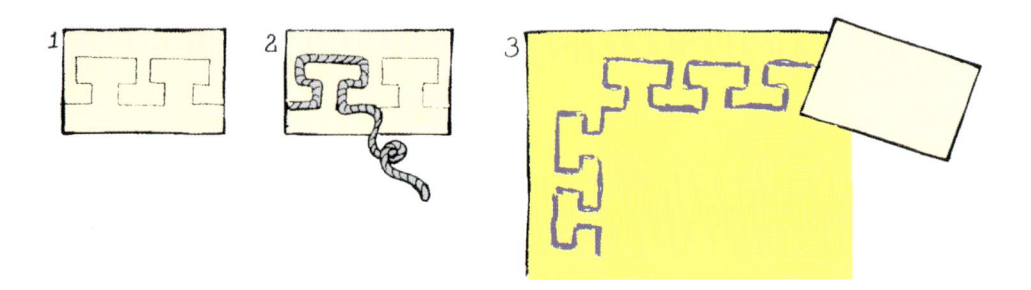

Make a Green Packet for Hari Raya Eidil Fitri

Materials: An A5 sheet of green paper. Scissors and glue. Gold paint pen or gold stickers (for decoration). Coins, notes or sweets for filling the packet.

Instructions: Fold the paper in half, then flatten out lengthwise so that the fold mark is showing in the middle. Cut away a narrow strip from the right outer edge to the middle, leaving the left half higher to form the flap of the envelope. On the right side, cut a small strip away from the side and the bottom half (approx. 1cm), so that the left side is wider and deeper. Fold in half. Fold the left overhanging outer and bottom edges over the right side. Tuck behind and glue to form a packet. Decorate the packet with a gold paint pen or sticker. You can write *'Selamat Hari Raya Eidil Fitri'* or 'Happy Hari Raya' on it if you like. Fill the envelope with money or sweets, then glue down the flap and give it to someone special!

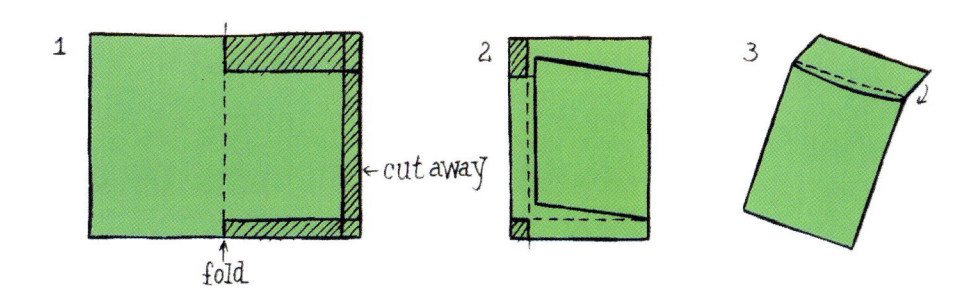

Gateway to Singapore Culture

How much do you really know about your classmates and neighbours? What do you know about the traditions of your own community? Read and find out!

150x210mm, 96pp, full colour,

ISBN 981-229-385-X.

Publisher
ASIAPAC BOOKS PTE LTD
996 Bendemeer Road #06-09 Singapore 339944
Tel: (65) 63928455 Fax: (65) 63926455
Email asiapacbooks@pacific.net.sg

Come visit us at our Internet home page
www.asiapacbooks.com

This edition
First published October 2005

© 2005 ASIAPAC BOOKS, SINGAPORE
ISBN 981-229-418-X
© All rights reserved

Printed in Singapore by FuIsland Offset Printing